THE SW

AND

ITS NEIGHBOURS

ROY LEWIS

Stafford Street Series 2

First Edition 2005
Second (revised) Edition 2009

ISBN 978-0-9553807-9-2

Published by Roy Lewis,
8 Tamar Grove
Western Downs
Stafford ST17 9SL

INTRODUCTION

This book traces the history of each building and its occupants from number 36 to number 46 Greengate Street, in the same way that number 1 in the series, 'From High House to Baker's Oven', traced the histories of numbers 47 to 58. It might have been titled 'From Chetwynd House to Shaw's House'.

Almost all the accounts start in the early eighteenth century, at a time when the old timber-framed houses that had stood on these sites since the sixteenth century or earlier were being replaced by brick buildings. Much of this part of Greengate Street was then taken up by large houses for professional people. The book also describes their later conversion into shops and banks.

Properties were not numbered until 1850, but in these pages numbers have been used at earlier dates in order to identify buildings. Sources before 1850, not having the benefit of numbers, often fail to make clear which property they refer to and mis-identification is an ever present risk. Incomplete evidence, such as the intervals between directories, can lead to a margin of error of one or two years in dates quoted in this book. This applies to modern as well as older dates.

My thanks go to the staffs of The William Salt Library, the Staffordshire Record Office, and the Staffordshire County Library for assistance and advice and to numerous individuals who have shared information with me and made helpful suggestions.

NOTE TO SECOND EDITION

This is largely a reprint of the first edition of 2005, updated to account for the changes in the occupation of properties in the last four years. During those years ongoing research has firmed up some dates and confirmed or modified some conjectures. It has also pushed back the beginnings of the stories of numbers 35 and 41, and filled in gaps in the histories of numbers 37, 38 and 44. This new information has been incorporated into the text.

Many of those who appear in the following pages are but names. The growing enthusiasm for tracing family histories will almost certainly lead to more detailed information being discovered about some of them. I am always grateful to those who share this information with me and allow it to be incorporated in a possible third edition.

ROY LEWIS

February 2009

NUMBER THIRTY SIX - CHETWYND HOUSE

John Chetwynd of Ingestre was a member of one of the county's oldest landowning families. Until his death in 1693 he was one of the two M.P.s Stafford sent to Parliament. His eldest son Walter inherited the Ingestre estate, was chosen as M.P. to succeed his father and was appointed High Steward of the town. Walter's youngest brother, William, after leaving Oxford University, took up a minor government appointment as secretary to the British Envoy in Turin and, later, became British Envoy in Genoa. He returned to England in 1712 and in 1715 he and his brother Walter were elected as the two M.P.s for Stafford.

Chetwynd House about 1900

On the corner of Mill Bank was a large, old timber-framed house. In 1681 it was owned by William Feake, a goldsmith living in Market Square, and let to Edward Foden, gentleman. Feake had also leased from the Corporation for 99 years a walled court or garden in front of the house, described as 'lately taken out of Greengate Street'. When Feake died in 1696, his son inherited the property and continued to let it to Edward Foden. William Chetwynd bought the property from him at some date between 1712, when Chetwynd returned to England, and 1715, when he married Honora Baker, daughter of the British Consul in Algiers, who brought him a considerable dowry.

William Chetwynd demolished the old house and in its place built a town house fit for the town's M.P. and his new bride. His new house was a large red brick building with prominent stone pilasters at each corner, giving it an elegant, symmetrical frontage to Greengate Street. The interior had fine oak panelled rooms and a handsome staircase that rose from the hall to the upper floors. The small courtyard in front (leased from the Corporation until the freehold was bought in 1818) was enclosed with iron railings and had a wrought iron gateway with the initials W C intertwined. Behind the house was a walled garden with lawns and gravelled walks. A small fountain was fed from a tank in the roof of the house. There were clumps of trees and bushes

William and his brother were both Whigs who supported the Hanoverian kings. In 1717 William was appointed to a government post as a Lord Commissioner of the Admiralty. In the election of 1722 he was defeated at

Stafford and an anti-Whig mob attacked his house. However, he remained in the government as M.P. for the naval constituency of Plymouth. He was again elected at Stafford in 1734 and retained the seat until his death in 1770.

In 1744 he was appointed to the lucrative post of Master of the Mint, a post once held by Sir Isaac Newton. In 1745 he entertained the Duke of Cumberland at Chetwynd House, when the King's army marched through Staffordshire after pursuing Bonnie Prince Charlie and his invading army of Scots.

In 1747 the parliamentary election was a violent affair in many places. In Stafford, William Chetwynd and his house were the prime target. On the evening of July 1st, a few days before polling began, many of the public houses were serving free drinks at the expense of the candidates. A noisy group assembled in the market place, hoisted a man on their shoulders, and proclaimed him "The Bishop". Then, preceded by morris dancers and a drummer, they paraded down Greengate Street, attracting a noisy, excited mob as they went. By the time they reached Chetwynd House, the mob numbered about 150. Mud was thrown at the windows and admission to the courtyard in front of the house demanded. Peter Dudley, Chetwynd's porter, barred the way at the gates.

Then the mood turned ugly. Someone fetched large stones to throw at the windows, which were soon smashed, except in the attics which the heavy stones did not reach. John Birtles, a cheesemonger, with others behind him, knocked Peter Dudley down, invaded the courtyard, and broke down the front door. Some 30 or 40 of the mob crowded into the house. Furniture was broken, a looking glass smashed and the wainscot damaged. William Chetwynd, with his family and friends who had been dining there, took refuge in the attics in fear for their safety. Then Edward Feepound, a J.P., had the Riot Act read and the mob gradually calmed down and, within half an hour, had left the house. Eighteen of the mob were later arrested and sent for trial, but Chetwynd decided not to press charges.

William Chetwynd had a swarthy complexion. He was nicknamed "Orinoco" Chetwynd by his political enemies. His wife had died in childbirth as early as 1726 and he divided his time between Stafford and London, where he was regularly seen in the highest social circles. He was always an energetic and active man. At the age of 80 he could still dance into the early hours at county balls held in the Shire Hall and preferred to ride horseback to London rather tha take a coach. As he grew older, he became estranged from his children. At the age of 83 he inherited the title Viscount Chetwynd and died three years later, leaving Chetwynd House to his grandson, named William after his grandfather.

This William Chetwynd was still a child and, after 1770, the house was let to a series of tenants. The first of these was either Edward Whitby, a lawyer who had been Recorder of Stafford, or his son of the same name. In 1782 the house was let to Ellen Byrd, the unmarried daughter of John Byrd of Milford Hall. Byrd had no sons. His elder daughter inherited Milford Hall and married the Rev. Richard Levett. When she died late in 1784 giving birth to her fifth child, Ellen went to live at Milford Hall to look after the children and manage her brother-in-law's household.

After remaining vacant for more than a

a year, Chetwynd House was let to William Horton. Horton, born in 1750, was the son of a Stafford shoemaker. In the 1770s he had established the first large scale manufacture of of shoes in the town. Large numbers of outworkers were employed to produce thousands of pairs of shoes in stock sizes. These were sold wholesale to the army or to dealers in London and other populous places. Horton became wealthy and the visible sign of his wealth was his occupation of Chetwynd House.

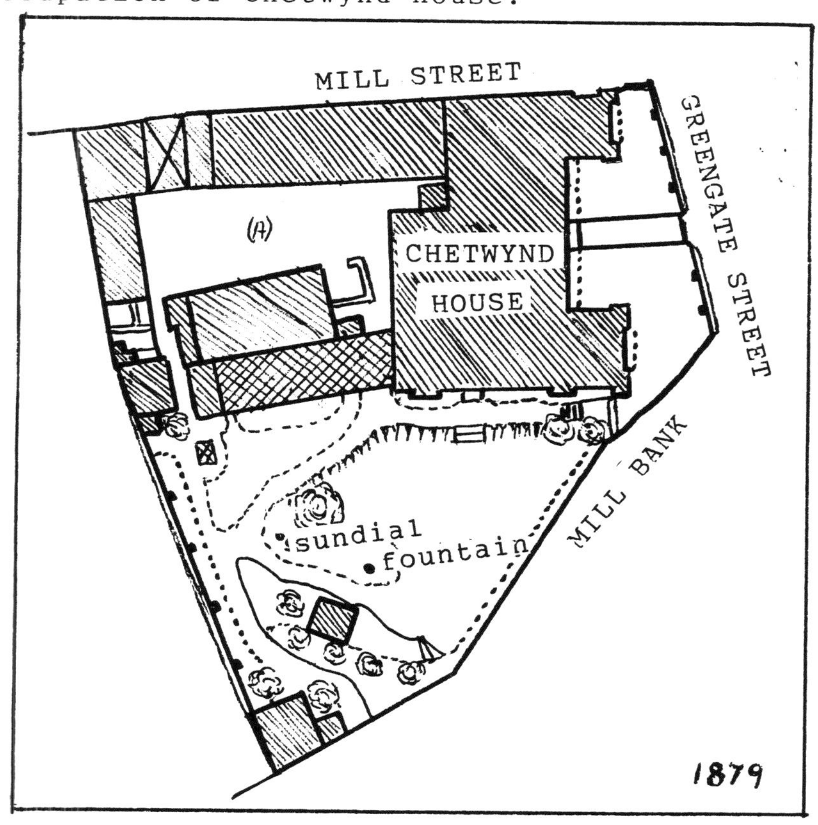

Plan of Chetwynd House showing Horton's shoe manufactory (A).

He converted a courtyard and outbuildings at the rear, with an arched-over entrance from Mill Street, into the hub of his business. Leather was stored there and cut out ready for collection by the outworkers who sewed the shoes. Finished shoes were brought back to be inspected before the workers were paid. During the Napoleonic wars, Thomas Bell, the chief buyer of shoes for the army, 'purchased from my friend Mr Horton £1,000 worth of shoes at a time'. William Collier, another shoe manufacturer, estimated that in the early 1800s Horton employed almost a thousand men, women and children and made £75,000 worth of shoes a year. In later years the volume of trade declined and most of Horton's output was sold in Manchester and Liverpool.

Horton was a Whig and, while he lived there, Chetwynd House continued to be the focus for local Whigs, as it had been in William Chetwynd's day. Richard Brinsley Sheridan, playwright and M.P. for Stafford, was always welcome there. In London he was in perpetual financial difficulty and relied on Horton's "gifts". In return Sheridan introduced Horton to those who might forward Horton's business, and brought his London friends to add to social life at Chetwynd House.

James Amphlett, who lived in Stafford, wrote, 'William Horton, the prince of presidence and amphytron of the borough, was the marked man of the county town and received all the wits and bright spirits of the age coming in the train of Sheridan. Horton was the presiding genius of the house; his brother John was the Bacchus and custos of the wine closet and sang an excellent song. Private society in Stafford took an elevated distinction in the county. There were six ladies who were styled the illustrious groupe and their elegant hospitalities attracted general notice; there was also a galaxy of other beauties.' The horse races held each year on Coton Fields evolved into Race Week, with balls and parties as well as racing. During Race Week, Sheridan usually stayed at Chetwynd House and twice, in the 1790s, brought his friend the Prince Regent with him. Chetwynd House still has a Sheridan Room but the story that "The School for Scandal" was written there is unfortunately untrue. The play was first performed in 1777, years before Horton moved into the house.

Sheridan ceased to be M.P. for the town in 1806 and his visits to Chetwynd House came to an end. Horton continued to live there until he died in 1832, but by then the house had ceased to be the social centre of the town.

William Horton had no children, but his brother John had a daughter, Elizabeth, who was always William's favourite. She married Edward Knight, the son of the vicar of Milwich. He had studied medicine at Edinburgh and in 1808 returned to Stafford as a physician at the infirmary. In 1809 he enlisted in the army and accompanied troops on the disastrous Walcheren expedition. At the end of the war, he retired with a pension and the rank of lieutenant-colonel. After he married Elizabeth Horton, William Horton invited them to live at Chetwynd House and their first-born son, John Horton Knight, was born there in 1826.

Knight built up an extensive private practice in the town. He became honorary physician to the infirmary, the gaol, and

Coton Hill Hospital. In 1842 he wrote a report on the sanitary state of Stafford for a Parliamentary Inquiry. He became a member of the town council and a magistrate. In 1822 he was chosen as mayor.

Horton had bought the freehold of Chetwynd House in 1827 and about the same time took his foreman in the shoe manufacture into partnership as Horton & Turner. After he died, Edward Knight and his family went on living in Chetwynd House, and Horton & Turner continued to manufacture shoes in premises behind the house.

Edward Knight.

Horton & Turner closed in the 1840s and the premises were offered on lease to other shoe manufacturers. In 1865 David Hollin set up his first shoe manufacturing business there with capital provided by Zachariah Anderson. As the use of machinery in the industry increased the premises became out-of-date and in 1874 David Hollin moved to a new factory in Rowley Street built to his own specifications. In 1880 Adams & Rowlands tried to start a small factory in Horton's old premises but went bankrupt in 1882.

Edward Knight lived at Chetwynd House until he died in 1862 at the age of 82. He had taken Edward Frederick Weston into partnership in his medical practice. Edward Weston married Edward Knight's daughter and they lived at Chetwynd House from 1862 until 1881. During those years a dispute arose between the Westons and other descendants of Edward Knight about the division of his estate. This dragged on until 1880, when the Court of Chancery ordered all the property, including Chetwynd House, to be sold by auction. Before the auction took place, Major John Knight, Edward Knight's son, bought Chetwynd House privately. Edward Weston and his wife moved to Green Hall on the Lichfield Road and Major Knight moved into Chetwynd House.

Major Knight had also bought the shoe manufactory at the rear of the house. The old buildings were of little value. In the 1870s Thomas Sproston had used part of them as a workshop and store for his cabinet making business but he moved to 21 Greengate Street before 1880. In the 1890s Walter Rooper, an electrical engineer and contractor, had an office and store there. Other businesses rented them for short periods as stores, but from about 1900 the buildings were vacant and semi-derelict.

In 1890 Major Knight let the house to the brothers Charles and George Reid. Both were Scots who had qualified as doctors at Aberdeen. George Reid had come to Stafford about 1876 as assistant to Edward Weston. Later, he became Medical Officer to Stafford Rural District Council and, in 1890, to Staffordshire County Council and its Education Department. His brother had a large private practice and was especially active in promoting the work of the British Red Cross Society.

When the Reids moved out in 1895, Edward Weston returned for a short time before the house was let to another doctor and surgeon, S. Butler. He remained at Chetwynd House until he died in 1909. The house was then left vacant and offered for sale.

At that time Stafford Post Office was in Market Square. Its premises were universally acknowledged to be too cramped and the Post Office was looking for larger premises into which they could move when their lease of the Market Square building expired in 1914. When it was announced that they had bought Chetwynd House, there was strong opposition from those who feared that the building would be extensively altered and its historic character lost.

In fact, the Post Office made little change to the exterior, apart from removing the attic windows and stripping ivy from the front. Inside, there was more change. The original main staircase was taken out and presented to South Kensington Museum. Other-

The new Post Office. Top - decorated for the official opening in March 1914. Bottom - the interior in 1914.

wise care was taken to preserve as much as possible of the original interior. As late as 1948 a visitor wrote, 'In the Post Master's room (on the left with a bow window) the oak panelling and door have been retained intact along with the original fireplace. Sheridan's room (ground floor on the right) is substantially as it was in his day and in the summer of this year will be opened up to the public. In the public office the oak beams spanning the ceiling are those installed when the building was erected'. Most of Horton's old shoe manufactory was pulled down to make a yard for vehicles to park and load. During the demolition a number of penny tokens, issued by William Horton to pay his workers, were discovered.

In the years after World War II the business of the Post Office increased rapidly, extensive internal reorganisation and a new side entrance became necessary. In October 2007, as part of a national reorganisation of Post Office services, the premises ceased to be a post office and were put up for sale. The new town post office was sited on the first floor of W.H.Smith's shop in Greengate Street. Externally, the property has remained much as it was when built by William Chetwynd in the early eighteenth century.

NUMBERS THIRTY SEVEN TO FORTY BEFORE 1760

If you had stood at the corner of Mill Street and Greengate Street in the early seventeenth century, you would have seen a medium sized, half-timbered house facing Greengate Street near the corner and, beyond it, a smaller cottage. Looking up Mill Street - it was then part of Earl Street - you would have noticed a barn and smelt the midden at the far end of it. Beyond these were more cottages, belonging to Lord Stafford. Much of the land near the Greengate Street cottage and the verges along Earl Street were town land belonging to the Corporation.

The house on the corner belonged to William Wolrich, a plumber. His daughter Joan had married an ironmonger, George Fowler, and in 1642 William sold the house to his son-in-law. George Fowler was a well-to-do tradesman. He was a town alderman and was chosen as mayor in 1652. After Joan died, he remarried and by his second wife had a daughter Anne. She inherited the house when her father died in February 1669.

In 1672 she married Humphrey Perry, a lawyer in Stafford, and they came to live in the house. Perry was a member of a wealthy Bilston family. He became a member of the Stafford town council and was chosen as mayor in 1692 and again in 1699. Anne bore him a son John in 1674, but in October 1675 died in childbirth. Her daughter, christened Joan, survived but died of smallpox in the following May. Humphrey Perry remarried in 1679; his second wife being the daughter of William Abnett, a neighbour in Greengate Street. She had no children and died in a coach accident in 1708. In the same year, Humphrey Perry's only son, John, died of smallpox.

In 1711 Perry bought the house adjoining the one where he lived and has left notes about its history. He wrote that in 1635 the corporation had leased a plot of town land with a cottage on it to Alice Allen for 99 years. She assigned her lease to Ralph Collins in 1637. Ralph and his wife Ursula lived there until the late 1670s, when the property was inherited by their son Ralph junior. About 1680 he sold it to William Ranshaw, who obtained a new 99 year lease from the corporation. Ranshaw also renewed Ralph Collin's lease of a barn in Earl Street behind the cottage.

By 1681 William Ranshaw had demolished down the cottage and built a new and larger brick house in its place. This is almost certainly the property which is numbers 39 and 40 Greengate Street today. He was mayor in 1701 and died in 1704, leaving a widow and a daughter Mary. His new house was left to his widow for her lifetime and then to his daughter. Mary married Thomas Fletcher. After she inherited the house in 1708, she and her husband mortgaged it to Walter Chetwynd for £100. In August 1711 they sold it to Humphrey Perry, who paid off the mortgage. He also acquired several pieces of town land - 'a piece of waste ground along Earl Street between the house and the barn, the garden at the mill, and a slang of land along my house from the enclosed by pales to the front of my house on the street side, with pales upon it.' The house Perry had bought from Thomas Fletcher was larger and more modern than his other house next to it. He probably moved next door from 1711 until his death in 1716 and let his other house to Ric Mountford.

When he died, he had no close relatives

to inherit and both houses, as well as all Perry's furniture, were acquired by his nephew William Robins. Robins was a prominent figure in the town and was chosen mayor in 1719, 1731 and 1740. He died in 1744, leaving a son John and two daughters, Catherine and Jane. There is a memorial to him and his family in St. Mary's church.

His son John had qualified as a barrister and had chambers in London, but spent most of his time in Stafford, where he lived with his father. He commanded a company of militia in the town at the time of the invasion by Bonny Prince Charlie and his army of Scots, was chosen as mayor in 1743 and elected M.P. for Stafford in 1747. He was then unmarried and almost forty years old.

John Whitby of Oakedge, a house on the edge of Cannock Chase, had died of smallpox in 1751, leaving a young widow with two small children. A contemporary described the widow as having 'eyes that were large, blue, languishing and full of love.' She had also inherited a substantial fortune. Numerous suitors courted her, but the one she favoured was John Robins. Early in 1752 he and Anne Whitby signed a contract stating that, although it was not convenient to solemnise a marriage at that time, they acknowledged themselves to be as husband and wife. A marriage should have followed shortly but Robins delayed.

Sir William Wolseley, a gentleman in his sixties, was infatuated with Anne and on 23 Sept 1752 married her in secret at Colwich. Anne later claimed that, while she was visiting the vicarage that day, she had been given a drugged drink by the vicar's wife and could not remember going through a marriage ceremony or signing a contract giving Wolseley control of her fortune.

On 7 October Robins married Anne Whitby at Castlechurch but, hearing rumours of a secret marriage, persuaded the vicar to enter the marriage in the parish register as having taken place on June 16th. Whispers of bigamy began to spread and Robins went to court to obtain a declaration that he was Anne's legal husband. The Vicar of Castlechurch then confessed to his bishop that he had falsified the parish register. Sir William Wolseley filed a suit for divorce and John Robins found himself facing charges of perjury. He fled abroad to escape the scandal and died there in1754 with large debts.

In his will, Robins left much of his property to his attorney, John Hichen, in trust to sell it to pay his debts. The rest of the estate was left to his sisters, the unmarried Jane Robins and Catherine, the wife of Brooke Crutchley, living in the High House. John Hichen bought the future number 39/40, where John Robins had lived The purchase money and the money raised by selling the future number 37/38, then let to Thomas Pigeon, was used to pay off some of Robins' extensive debts.

Hitchen lived in the house until his death in 1763. His executors sold the property to Jane Robins. As well as the house, there was a 4 foot wide strip of land along the Greengate Street frontage fenced with pales to give added security and privacy to the property, a rear yard and stable with access to Mill Lane, and two pews in St Mary's church, one in the front row of the gallery for Jane's own use and the other for her servants.

The separate histories of numbers 37/38 and 39/40 are related in the following pages.

NUMBER THIRTY SEVEN / THIRTY EIGHT

John Robins property on the corner of Mill Lane was bought by James Godwin, who continued to let it. Until 1771 the tenant was John Savage, gentleman, followed by Captain Francis Collier until 1784 and - Wilkinson briefly in 1784/5. During these years the old timber-framed house was rebuilt as a pair of smaller dwellings, with the front room of the corner house (the future 37) intended as a shop. The rebuilding had probably taken place by 1780, when a sketch map (drawn about 1800 but claiming to show premises in 1780) marks 'Captain Collier's houses' in the plural. It is also possible that rebuilding took place in 1785.

From 1785 to 1788 the corner shop was let to Richard Dale, a grocer and dealer in tea. In 1788 bakery ovens were built at the rear of the premises and Jonathan Adams opened a bakery there. About 1791 he moved to premises near the river.

James Godwin then sold both houses to another baker, John Wilkes. Wilkes moved into the corner shop (37) and let the other house (38). The tenant was probably Abraham Ward, a member of the family which leased the town mill, and later Samuel Croxton. He left in 1795.

The history of number 38 continues on page 21 : the story of number 37 continues below.

In 1795 John Wilkes retired, leaving his son William to carry on the bakery and live at number 37. At that time the weight, quality and price of loaves was still regulated by the old Assize of Bread. When wheat was plentiful the law was enforced very loosely

However, in the 1790s poor harvests resulted in shortages. Prices of bread and flour rose. In 1795, during a particularly severe shortage, the magistrates in Stafford, fearing disturbances in the town, enforced the Assize. William Wilkes was one of several bakers fined for selling loaves that were not of standard size and quality. In 1800 a similar shortage did lead to riots against the price of bread. Wilkes and other bakers had their windows smashed and their shops looted. Order was only restored when a troop of light dragoons rode into Stafford and began patrolling the streets.

William Wilkes carried on the bakery until he died in 1834 and his widow, Joanna, continued the business until 1850, when she retired. She sold the business to Richard Marklow, a baker from Great Haywood. He lived above the shop with his family, a live-in journeyman baker and an errand boy.

In July 1858 Marklow let the premises and business to William Ward on a yearly tenancy. There is evidence that the business began to fall off during the following years. In 1863 Ward was given notice to quit and a year later moved into a shop in Gaol Square. In July 1864 Marklow himself re-opened his 'original home-baking and cottage loaf establishment, which will maintain the celebrity which the firm of Wilkes enjoyed for many years in the same premises'. He failed to halt the decline and in 1866 let the business to Mr Benton, and a year later to Thomas Billington, who stayed for four years. In 1871 George Stonier became the tenant and the business began to revive. When Richard Marklow died in 1877 his executors put both number 37 and 38 up for sale by auction. The freehold was probably bought by Albert Hammersley, a baker. In 1878 Stonier moved to Eastgate Street.

Albert Hammersley moved in and opened his bakery and confectionery shop in November 1878. He employed two men and a boy in the bakery as well as an assistant in the shop.

In 1897 John Greatbach bought the shop with the intention of expanding and diversifying the business. His shop sold biscuits, sweets and chocolates of every description, foreign and British wines; pork pies were a speciality and bride cakes were made to order. Greatbach also catered for family parties and school treats, offering a large tent and two portable boilers for hire on such occasions. The business did not thrive and he left in 1899. He was followed by Arthur Crinean, the last baker and confectioner to have his shop there. He moved to 46 Greengate Street in 1903.

In 1903 the shop was bought by Arthur Dobson, who had grown up in Stockton-on Tees. When he left school, he had started work in a tobacco factory in Leeds. By 1903 he was a commercial traveller covering the Midlands for a large cigar and tobacco manufacturer. He advertised that his new shop sold everything for the smoker. For pipe smokers, he had his own Greengate mixture of tobacco in three different strengths. The picture on page 20 shows his advertisement painted on the side wall of his shop. His business expanded and a second, larger shop was opened in Gaolgate Street. An extensive wholesale trade was also carried on. After he died in 1925, his sons Arthur and Leslie turned the business into a limited company, which continued to expand. F.W.Wile's cigar and tobacco shop in Market Square was taken over in 1933 and in the late 1940s a new wholesale warehouse was opened in North Walls. Advertisements proclaimed that the company was 'the leading tobacconist of the county town.'

In the late 1960s Arthur and Leslie Dobson retired and the shop closed. It was small, with windows that had not changed since 1903, or earlier. Those intending to open a new shop wanted more modern premises. After remaining vacant for some time, the shop opened as an Oxfam charity shop in the 1970s. In 1980 it was taken over by Voluntary Social Aid, who also had a charity shop there.

In 1988 the premises began a new life as a small clothes shop called Second Gear. In the late 1990s it became Baird's ladies' and children's clothing shop. After Baird's closed in 2001, the premises remained vacant until June 2002, when the Katherine House charity opened their Collectables shop there.

Greengate Street in 1910, numbers 37-8 centre.

NUMBER THIRTY EIGHT

After John Wilkes bought the future number 38, he let the house to the widow of Charles Kent, who lived there until 1806. After she left, George Sommerville, an attorney and the brother of Dr Henry Sommerville, moved in and stayed until about 1818.

When he moved out, John Coates, a shoe maker and repairer, used the front room as a shop where he could be seen working in the window. He lived there until 1856, when he was almost 70 years old. The front room was then refitted as a drapery and millinery shop by Charles Walker, who had just given up his shop in the High House. In the autumn of 1856 he advertised a sale of his remaining stock of summer millinery at 30% below cost and reminded customers of his stock of French corsets, collars, infants robes, skirts, caps, handkerchiefs and other drapery. In October 1859 he moved to a larger shop next to the Swan.

The next tenant was Joseph Marsh, who had an existing drapery and millinery shop in part of the High House and planned this as an extension of his business. The venture was not a success and closed a year later. Marsh seems to have sub-let the living accomodation over the shop to Joseph Cook, a druggist's assistant.

In December 1860 Henry Smethurst, born at Hume near Manchester, opened a watch and jewellery shop at number 38. For some months he continued to sub-let to Joseph Cook, but he seems to have moved into the living quarters above the shop before the end of 1861. His advertisements guaranteed that, if any watch bought at his shop was not approved of, it could be returned for a refund during the first year. He quickly established a reputation as a skilful watchmaker. After he died in January 1907, his son Charles took over the shop and expanded the jewellery side of it. Many of his advertisements refer to it as 'The Little Ring Shop'. In 1914 the business was transferred to larger premises on the other side of Greengate Street.

Number 38 remained a watch and jewellery shop. The new occupiers were Tom Pear & Son, who also owned a shop in Marston Road. After the 1914-18 War, Tom Pear's son continued to trade there as G.Pear (Stafford) Ltd until about 1930, when the shop became 'Modern Jewellers'. In 1938 Arthur Rhead acquired the premises and his watchmaker's and jeweller's shop remained there until 1952.

In 1953 the shop was refitted as Sneekers Shoe Salon, specialising in children's and ladies' fashion shoes. The shop was small with seats for no more than eight customers. A thorough modernisation was carried out in 1958, when the showroom was enlarged by taking in other rooms. The refurbished shop provided seats for up to 15 ladies as well as a children's corner with three seats raised on a low platform. Behind the seats was a colourful mural with two deer wearing jackets marked "Clarke's Shoes". Later in the year, a new gentlemen's department was added. A reporter quoted the manager as saying, 'Most people are prepared to pay £3 or more for a good pair of shoes.' In the 1960s the shop, still selling Clarke's shoes, became Harris' Shoes and, about 1970, Peter Lord Footwear. It closed as a shoe shop in 1987.

Warehouse Clearance occupied the premises temporarily, until the shop re-opened as Gigi Ladies' Fashions in 1989. Gigi closed in 1999 and, after a major refurbishment, Toni and Guy, hairdressers, opened their salon there.

THIRTY NINE (AND NUMBER 40 UP TO 1832)

In 1764 Jane Robins bought her brother's er's large house that would become numbers 39 and 40 at a later date. Like all houses built about 1700, it was planned symmetrically with a central front door. This led directly into a large hall 11½ feet wide and 27 feet long from door to the main staircase. John Robins had always dined in this room, sitting at either the large oval table or a smaller cedar wood table. The principal living rooms were either side of the hall - two parlours (one used as Jane's sitting room), a drawing room and John Robins' study, where he had transacted all his business. Each of these rooms was about 20 feet square. Behind them was the servants part of the house - kitchen, pantry, brewhouse and servants' hall - with a second staircase. On the upper floors were bedrooms, a disused nursery, and attic rooms for the servants. Outside, was a garden with gravelled walks and a summerhouse. The garden extended to Mill Street where there were stables for several horses.

Jane lived there until her death at the age of 82 in 1795. She is buried in the chancel of St Mary's church, where there is a memorial tablet to her and other family members. In her will, Jane left her house to her two nieces Catherine and Anne Crutchley. Neither lived in Stafford. Catherine, unmarried, lived at Shenstone Lodge near Lichfield, and Anne had married Edward Dickenson of Dosthill House near Tamworth. They let the house to Archibald Campbell, an elderly doctor, who had been physician at The Staffordshire General Infirmary for many years. He had been mayor in 1780 and 1792 and would serve a third term in 1801. In 1802 he bought the house from Anne Dickenson and Catherine Crutchley. He died in 1805 and his widow sold the property to William Collier.

William Collier was a tanner. He was also the adjutant of the Loyal Stafford Vounteers and had written their manual of military movements. In 1807, in partnership with William Ford, he started manufacturing shoes wholesale, with a warehouse in Mill Street. In January 1807 the partners were recruiting 200 outworkers, four good clickers to cut out leather, 'an experienced traveller to sell shoes and a few young men, able to give sureties, to fix shoes in manufacturing towns'. After Ford withdrew in 1808, Collier carried on alone. At first the business prospered and his weekly wage bill reached £150. Then trade became depressed. The wage bill fell to £20 a week and in 1811 Collier was forced to sell his house and move into a smaller property next door.

The new owner was Henry Sommerville, a doctor, who was chairman of the management committee at the Infirmary. In 1815 he sold the house to Anne Dickenson, now a widow, who was seeking to return to Stafford. Before she moved in, the house was redecorated and refurbished. The bedroom over the hall was turned into a fashionable sitting room and one of the outhouses converted into a cowhouse so that Anne could have fresh milk daily. She died in November 1818 and the house was sold by auction the following January.

The house was bought by George Keen, the younger brother and partner of William Keen of Rowley Hall, the leading attorney in the town. William Keen died in 1828 after being kicked by a horse in his stable yard at the Hall. He left the Hall to his brother George.

George moved into Rowley Hall and seems to have divided his Greengate Street house into two dwellings. The larger and more southerly of them (number 39) he sold to Dr John Garratt in 1830. Garratt lived there until he died in 1841. The history of the other dwelling (number 40) is told on page 26.

The future number 39 was bought by Charles Morgan, a wine and spirit merchant. His father, Thomas Morgan, had left Stoke-on-Trent in 1806 to take over a wholesale and retail wine business in Stafford. Charles was made a partner in the early 1820s and took over the business when his father retired in 1827. Morgan's wine vaults were then in Martins Place, opposite the judges' lodgings. Charles Morgan invested heavily in early railway shares, which he later sold at a very great profit and became a wealthy man.

He bought number 39 as a home for his family; his business remained in Martins Place. In 1846 he bought and rebuilt 57 Greengate Street as his main place of business. He also bought The Roebuck in Greengate Street and The Star in the market place. He was for many years a town councillor and alderman and was mayor in 1845. One of the tradesmen in the town, who knew him well, described him as 'worldly wise'. When his wife died in the 1840s, a female cousin came to keep house for him. A cook and two maids lived-in and other servants came in daily. John, his older surviving son (his eldest son died in 1840 aged 10), became a partner in the wine merchants and his younger son William became a solicitor in the town. Charles moved to a more suburban house in 1860.

The house in Greengate Street was bought

by Charles Chester Mort and John Drewry Mort, the proprietors of The Staffordshire Advertiser. Number 39 ceased to be used as a dwelling and from 29 September 1860 The Advertiser was produced there. William Baker, who started work there about 1870, recalled that there was still a garden at the rear. During the 1870s new printing rooms were built in the garden, with a frontage to Mill Street, and printing presses installed there.

The Staffordshire Advertiser was produced there for almost a century. In 1955 the paper was bought by Powysland Newspapers Ltd, who merged it with The Staffordshire Chronicle and printed the combined paper out of town. In 1960 Amalgamated Securities bought the property and the paper moved to Salter Street.

Number 39 was then altered into a ground floor shop with offices on the upper floors. In the 1960s the shop was occupied by Dorothy Perkins Separates Ltd, sellers of ladies' clothes, who moved from number 2 Greengate Street. In 1978 further alterations converted the ground floor into two smaller shops. One of these was occupied by Smethurst & Son, jewellers and watchmakers, and the other let to Top Travel International Ltd. In the late 1990s Smethurst and Son closed and Top Travel International expanded into both shops. The company removed to Gaolgate Street at the end of 2000, and the premises remained vacant.

NUMBER FORTY AFTER 1832

The more northerly part of George Keen's house was leased to the Manchester and Liverpool District Bank, which opened its first

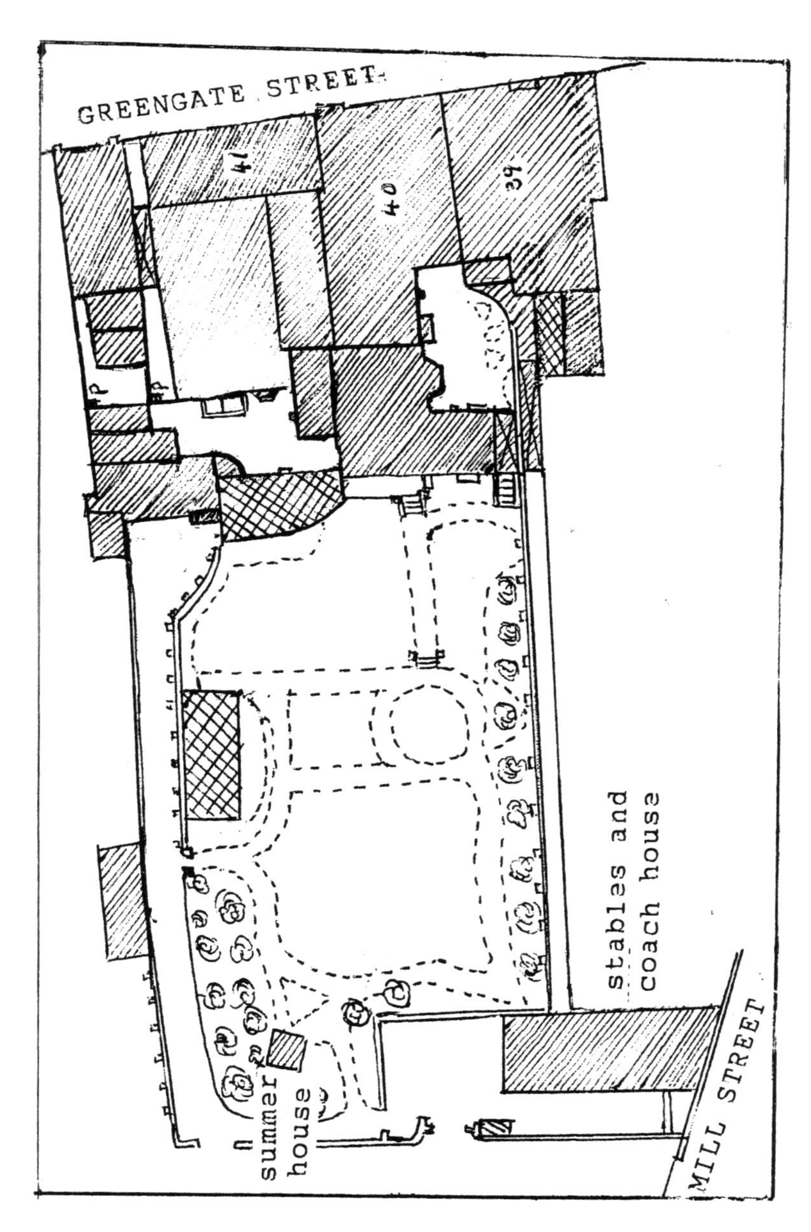

Numbers 39 to 41 in 1879.

Stafford branch there on 1 October 1832. The District Bank was one of the first joint-stock banks. Older banks had been partnerships of two or three well-to-do businessmen and their solvency depended on the reputation and credit worthiness of the partners. Joint-stock banks had shareholders and were much less likely to be declared bankrupt because of a loss of confidence causing a run on the bank.

The Manchester and Liverpool District Bank, formed in 1829, had almost a dozen branches in the north and midlands by 1832. Each branch had a local chairman with a board of directors of respected local people. They met weekly to manage the affairs of the branch. In Stafford the first chairman was Joseph Lovatt, a wine merchant; the other directors were Charles Morgan, living next to the bank; C.H.Webb, a solicitor; and Thomas Webb, a draper.

Birch & Yates, one of the old style banks, had been forced into bankruptcy after the death of Edmund Birch, one of the partners. When the affairs of the bank were finally settled in the summer of 1832, The District Bank bought the remaining assets and appointed Edmund Birch's son Edmund junior as its fist manager in Stafford.

The banking hall was at the front of the building with a new door onto Greengate Street. The chairman had his own room, where he received important clients, and where hospitality flowed freely. Rooms on the upper floors became the bank manager's house. The bank was an immediate success among local farmers and tradesmen, attracting clients like Thomas Bostock & Son and John Marson of the High House. In May 1834 the bank bought the freehold of the property, which had become known as Bank House. In November 1832 a one-day-a-week branch was opened in Rugeley, with one of the clerks driving over in the bank's gig. A second branch was opened in Stone a year later.

The bank expected irreproachable conduct from its employees. In 1837 one of the clerks, Mr Wolfenden, was suspended, 'having absented himself from the bank for two days and appeared before the magistrates of this borough for eloping with a married woman, the wife of a very respectable young man, at whose house he had lodged . . . and having outraged the feelings of the inhabitants of the town by his unprincipled conduct.'

By the 1860s more space was needed and the bank bought the adjoining house, number 41. This was demolished, and rebuilt in 1867 with the latest banking facilities. Number 40 became the bank manager's house with a communicating door into the new building. The bank's stable and coach house in Mill Street were also rebuilt. The plan on page 27 shows how the extensive gardens were combined. The new building had a small flat at the rear for a porter/night-watchman/ coachman. Thomas Bradbury was appointed to the post.

The managers who lived at Bank House before and after the changes were:- Edmund Birch (1832-5), George Webb (1835-43), Jonas Pilling (1843-74), William Sharp (1875-8), F. W. Hobson (1878-81) and Robert Cumming (1882-1906). Managers were encouraged to take other posts which brought additional business to the bank. Jonas Pilling was Secretary to The Stafford New Gas Light Company and brought their account to the bank. In 1883 Robert

Cumming was appointed as part-time Borough Treasurer and all the corporation accounts were handled at the bank. When Cumming retired in 1906, the town council decided that a full-time Borough Treasurer was needed and the bank that, in future, managers could live where they wished, rather than be forced to live at Bank House.

Number 40 had become redundant. The premises, including the stable block and the garden, which now had a tennis lawn, were put up for auction in May 1907 and sold for £2,000.

The new owners were Evans & Evans, estate agents and auctioneers, who moved from Phoenix Chambers in Market Square to their new office and saleroom in October 1907. Since then, new display windows and a new door have been put in. The original entrance being retained to provided a way through to the temporary buildings erected in the garden for use as sale rooms. In 1959 the stable block was sold to Peter Rogers, photographer, and converted into a shop.

In the 1990s the Bradford & Bingley Building Society took over the estate agents but retained the name Evans & Evans. In November 2004 the building society sold all its estate agencies to Countrywide, who also rettained the name Evans & Evans. In 2008 it became bridgfords.

FORTY ONE

This medium sized house fit for a professional man had been built in the early eighteenth century. It had a central hall flanked on one side by a drawing room and library and on the other by a dining room and a room that would be either office or consulting room. At the rear were the kitchen, brewhouse and pantry. There was a yard, a garden, stables and a coach house with a right of way to drive into Mill Street. The owner usually had the use of two pews in St Mary's church, one for himself and his family and the other for servants.

In the 1720s Edward Green lived here and may have built the house on the site of a smaller house once occupied by Christopher Cramer. Green was an attorney and Town Clerk of Stafford. He was chosen as mayor in 1723 and died in 1736. His widow continued to live in the house until her death in 1750. Their son Edward junior then inherited the house. He was living in Yorkshire and let the house to John Savage until 1764. He then sold it to John Buchanan, a physician with a large private practice. Buchanan was also physician at the infirmary from its opening in 1766 until his death in 1767. His widow lived there until 1784 when she retired to a smaller house and let the house in Greengate Street to William Keen, senior.

Keen was the foremost attorney in the town. He acted for the county magistrates both in court and on all county business, as well as having an extensive private practice among landowners and tradesmen. He died in 1789, only a few months before the owner Mrs Buchanan. Her executors sold the property to Rev Edward Meeke from Eccleshall, who let it to Edward Clarke, a gentleman with an estate at Rickerscote. In 1796 Clarke resigned from the town council, gave up his rented house in Greengate Street and went to live in his house in Rickerscote.

The next tenant was Henry Sommerville, a doctor who had come to Stafford as the junior partner of Dr John Masfen of Gaolgate Street. In 1811 the doctor moved from number 41 to number 40 and 41 was let to William Collier, a shoe manufacturer, who had been at number 40. Collier moved out in March 1815 after an auction sale of his surplus furniture. Henry Sommerville then bought the house from the widow of Edward Meeke and moved back into it. He stayed until his death in 1830.

In 1830 the house was bought by Charles Flint, a solicitor, whose previous home had been in Eastgate Street. In the 1820s he had led a legal challenge to the way members of the council were appointed. After the passing of The Municipal Corporations Act (1835) those seeking to reform local government in the town saw Flint as a symbol of a new order. Elections in 1836 were fought between those wanting to keep Francis Brookes, the existing town Clerk, in office and those who wished to replace him with Flint. Flint's supporters won.

When Flint died in 1857 his house was sold to Richard Palin, who converted it into offices. The upper floors were let to the Inland Revenue and a partnership of Spragg & Joyce, architects. The ground floor was rented to the Manchester and Liverpool District Bank, which made extensive alterations.

By 1865 the bank was in need of more space. It bought number 41, gave the tenants notice, and demolished the building. Robert Griffith, who combined a large private practice with the post of County Architect, was

The new District Bank in 1867.

commissioned to design the new building. When it opened in 1867, the new bank had a street frontage with three steep gables and windows with pointed arches and stone tracery. An observer described it as 'a curious mixture of styles, yet the general effect is most charming'. Inside the main door there were four steps up to a small landing and then another six steps up to the main floor level. This allowed the construction of a basement with barrel vaults, where the bank's books and business documents were stored. At the top of the steps, was a waiting room on the right and the manager's office on the left. This had a door which led directly into the manager's house at number 40. The door was bricked up in 1907 and only re-discovered during alterations in 1958.

Straight ahead, at the top of the steps, was the banking hall. This was 40½ feet long and 23 feet wide with a massive stone fireplace at each end. The hall rose to a ceiling of ornamental glass with a large cupola supported on oak beams. This was 29 feet above the floor of the hall. At the rear of the building was a lodge for a porter or coachman and a bedroom was provided above the strong room room, so that a member of staff could sleep on the premises if necessary. A room was also set aside for The Stafford Mutual Permanent Building Society, for which the bank acted as treasurer.

The District Bank (its title had been shortened) stayed largely as it had been built until 1958, when a lower false ceiling was put over the banking hall to conserve heat. A new flat roof with special heat insulation was put in at the same time. This work was carried out without closing the bank, so that for several months customers and staff were surrounded by internal scaffolding.

About 1970 the District Bank became part of The National Westminster Bank, which already had a branch at 43 Greengate Street. The old 1867 building at number 41 was demolished. When it had been rebuilt, it replaced the other branch, which was closed. NatWest, as it is now called, still occupies number 41.

NUMBER FORTY TWO

This was a much smaller house than its neighbours and little is known about its history. In the early eighteenth century it was generally known as Harding's House, after Richard Harding, a glazier, who died in 1701, leaving the house to his widow for life and then to his nephew Thomas Winkle. By 1732 Widow Winkle was living there. The Winkles owned the property until 1790, although they only lived there until 1780 when the house was let to Widow Sharkey. She had just sold a larger house next to The Swan. After her death in 1785, the house was let to Mr Nicholls and then to Rev Proctor.

When John Winkle, the grandson of Widow Winkle, died in 1790/1, he left the house to John Hughes of Radford, the owner of The Horn and Trumpet, for his lifetime, and then to Omar Hall and his wife. The Rev Proctor continued to live there as the tenant until 1807.

Omar Hall was a banker at 57 Greengate Street, using the same premises as his brother Joseph, who had a drapery shop there. In 1807, when Joseph became bankrupt, the property had to be sold. Omar moved out and gladly accepted John Hughes offer of the tenancy of number 42. The bank opened there in the spring of 1807, using one room as an office and banking hall. Omar applied successfully for a licence to issue his own £1 banknotes, which circulated locally and could be exchanged at his bank. In March thieves broke into the bank, broke open the great, iron-bound chest where notes were stored, and took about £2,000 of Omar's own notes and £700 in other notes and drafts. About £300, wrapped in a handkerchief, was recovered from a ditch by the side of the Wolverhampton road. A reward of £100 was offered but the thieves were not caught.

Confidence in the bank was shattered. Those who had money deposited there tried to withdraw it, but most of it was on loan so that Omar could not pay out in cash and was forced to close the doors of the bank. Two weeks after the robbery he was declared bankrupt. All his assets were sold at auction, including the reversion of number 42, which was bought by John Hughes himself. He allowed Omar to go on living there.

Omar's shares in the tramway that carried coal from the canal at Radford into Stafford had been sold when he became bankrupt. Now, he promoted a new scheme to straighten and canalise the river between the Green Bridge and Radford so that boats could bring coal directly into the town. Money was raised and the work started but Omar failed to make it clear that the canal company had not approved a lock to connect the canal to the river. Coal would have to be transferred from one boat to another at Radford. Omar left Stafford in 1811. When work on the river was completed in August 1812, townsmen realised that no lock would be built. The Corporation passed a resolution that his conduct was 'unworthy and improper'. In later years, Omar's fortunes sank even lower. In 1817 he was convicted of stealing a brace of fowls and transported to Australia.

After Omar Hall moved out, the house at number 42 became a small shop let to Elizabeth Bradley, a maker of straw hats. In July 1811 she moved into 'the house lately occupied by Mr Omar Hall.' She left in 1820 and for the next three years the premises were occupied by Miss Hughes, a dressmaker and relative of the owner.

Early in 1823 the property was let to John Bott, a tailor. His daughter Elizabeth had trained as a dressmaker. In June 1823, she started her own business in the same premises as her father. Ten years later, she sold the business, including all her patterns, to her senior assistant Caroline Shelton, who moved into a lock-up shop at The High House a few months later. John Bott continued his tailor's shop there until the late 1830s.

The property was then let to George Nevitt, a small-scale wholesale maker of boots and shoes. He sub-let the shop to Henry Jenkinson, a hairdresser living in The High House. In 1843 Jenkinson bought the property and George Nevitt moved out. About this time the house and shop were rebuilt, perhaps by Henry Jenkinson. The earliest photograph of Greengate Street in 1858 shows one corner of the new building on the far left, with Jenkinson's sign projecting from it. (See page 40).

After Henry Jenkinson died in August 1859, the premises were sold to Charles Wright, who opened a draper's shop in December 1859. In December 1864 he sold it to Josiah Hadley. Hadley had just dissolved his partnership with his brother Thomas, leaving Thomas with their Market Street shop. Josiah Hadley described himself as a woollen draper, hosier, outfitter and gentlemen's tailor. His advertised stock included woollen cloth, shirts, collars, ties, hosiery, umbrellas, men's tweed hats and silk hats. He stocked ready made garments in the latest styles and supplied made-to-measure suits from 50 shillings and trousers from 15 shillings and sixpence.

In 1876/7 Hadley made extensive alterations to the shop, putting in larger display windows on ground and first floors. His 'Stafford Emporium' reopened in February 1877. Business prospered and he moved to a Market Square shop in

1880. For the next few years number 42 was the parcels office for the Midland and Stafford to Uttoxeter railways.

In 1886 Henry and Joseph Deakin, tailors, moved into the shop from 44 Greengate Street. They stayed until about 1895, when they sold their business to Storer Bros. The tailoring shop closed in the early months of 1898.

The property was bought by the brothers E.A. and A.S. Thompson, who had been in business in Birmingham. In March 1898 they opened The Manchester and Bradford Warehouse at number 42. In 1907 they bought part of number 43 from Nash & Co, wine and spirit merchants, putting in a new display window and opening a fancy drapery department there. The postcard below shows numbers 42 and 43 in 1908.

In 1911 the Thompsons bought the rest of number 43, subject to existing leases of the top floor. When these expired in 1920, the whole building was refurbished and given four new display windows. Ernest Thompson became active in local government. He was elected onto the town council in 1921 and invited to become mayor in 1922. For many years he was chairman of the Markets Committee.

In the 1940s the business was sold to Haycock & Tooth. They sold off number 43 in 1954 but carried on trading at number 42 until the late 1960s. After remaining vacant for some time, the premises were bought by the Co-operative Bank. The bank has complet-ely rebuild the property and still occupies the building today.

The earliest photograph of Greengate Street, taken in 1858. The corner of number 42 with Jenkinson's sign on it can be seen on the far left.

NUMBER FORTY THREE

At the beginning of the eighteenth century the house on this site belonged to Humphrey Perry, an attorney in the town. He let it to his father-in-law William Abnett, who came from Audley and was mayor of Stafford in 1706. Katherine Abnett, Perry's second wife, died in 1708 after the horses in her coach took fright and bolted on Sandon Bank. The coachman was thrown from his box; the coach crashed into the bridge, and Katherine, suffering from 'fright and convulsions', was carried into The Dog and Doublet. She died a few days later.

When William Abnett moved out of the house in 1713, it was leased to John Tombes, Doctor of Philosophy, who had just come to live in the town and immediately been made a capital burgess and an alderman. After he died in 1729, his executor sub-let the house to Roger Venables, who stayed until he left the town in 1734. The house was then occupied by a succession of tenants - Rev William Loxdale, Widow Swinnerton and Captain Nicholls. In 1752 the house was sold to George Cookes, an attorney, who was appointed Town Clerk in 1766. He lived there until 1785.

William Withering, who had been the physician at The Staffordshire General Infirmary since 1767, bought the house in 1785, but, later the same year, was appointed physician at Birmingham General Hospital. He let the house to Mrs Moore, a widow, and later to Abraham Ward, the brother of John Ward, a surgeon at the infirmary. In 1795 Dr Withering sold the house to Francis Hughes, the son of Robert Hughes, the first apothecary and secretary to the board at the infirmary. Robert Hughes had assisted Dr Withering with his research into the medicinal use of digitalis and died in 1793 after picking up an infection while treating prisoners at the gaol. Francis Hughes had trained as a doctor and had a large private practice in the town. After his father's death, he took over his father's medical duties at both the infirmary and the gaol. He was the senior doctor in the town, took an active role in local government and was twice chosen as mayor. His sons Richard and Robert also became doctors. Robert, the younger brother, took over Francis' duties at the infirmary when his father retired in 1833. Richard, the older brother, became his father's partner in his private practice and moved into his father's house when Francis died in 1837. In the 1850s Richard suffered a stroke which left him partially paralysed and forced him to give up both the house and the practice.

The new owner of the house in 1856 was George Shields, an insurance agent, who had just been appointed postmaster. At that time postmasters were expected to provide their own post offices and number 43 was altered for that purpose. The earliest photograph of Greengate Street (page 40) shows number 43 as a doublefronted, two storey house with shallow bay windows either side a central door. The most northerly of the rooms fronting the street became the post office, with a room for sorting letters behind it. It is said that the town at that time had two postmen and a postwoman, who had a milk round as well as delivering letters. George Shields moved to Coventry in 1867 and the post office was removed to Market Square.

In 1867 the property was bought by Nash & Lienard, wine importers and merchants.The business sold foreign wines, liqueurs. and cigars as well as ale and porter in bottles and kegs. They were also the local agents for Bunting's Uttoxeter brewery. Most of their business was wholesale and, in addition to their Greengate Street premises, they rented cellars in Park Street and beneath The Waverley Temperance Hotel. Frederick Nash managed the Stafford shop and lived on the premises until the mid 1870s. Lienard retired soon after 1880 and the business was renamed Nash & Co. In the early twentieth century the business declined. The southern part of their premises was sold in 1907 and the rest in 1911 when the business closed.

The Manchester and Bradford Warehouse at number 42 expanded into number 43 in 1907 and again in 1911. The upper floor was then occupied by Madeleine Bostock's dental surgery, held on a lease that did not expire until 1920. When she left about 1914, the remainder of her lease was bought by Richard Nevitt, a surveyor and estate agent. As soon as the lease expired, The Manchester and Bradford Warehouse Company refurbished the whole building, making extensions at the rear and putting in new display windows.

The business was sold to Haycock & Tooth in the early 1940s. The new owners sold number 43 in 1954 but continued to trade at number 42. The upper floor of number 43 had been let to Evelyn Lewis as a ladies' and children's hairdressing salon. When she left it was let to Arthur Evans, an accountant and the local agent of The Leek and Moorland Building Society.

In 1954 The Leek and Moorland Building Society bought number 43 and put in a new ground floor frontage before opening their first Stafford branch office in the northern part, called 43A. The southern half was occupied by The Westminster Bank and known as number 43. The upper floor continued to be the offices of Arthur Evans until he retired about 1960. It then became the offices of Nowell, Mellor and Nowell, solicitors.

In 1968 The Westminster Bank amalgamated with The National & Provincial Bank. The new National Westminster Bank had two Greengate Street branches. The one at number 41 was rebuilt and when it re-opened in the early 1970s, the branch at number 43 became redundant and closed. About the same time Nowell, Mellor and Nowell moved into new offices at Oxford House.

The Leek and Moorland Building Society then completely rebuilt number 43 and occupied the whole building when it re-opened. The society, now renamed The Britannia Building Society, is still there.

NUMBER FORTY FOUR

In the seventeenth century this house next to The Swan was smaller than most other houses on the west side of Greengate Street. It was listed in the lowest band of properties for which Window Tax was payable in the 1690s. We can imagine it as a very ordinary two storey house with a timber frame infilled with wattle and daub and a workshop at the rear. In the 1690s it was the home of Walter Eaton, a cooper or maker of barrels. He lived there for upwards of 40 years and died about 1740. From 1740 to about 1780 the house was occupied by John Starkey, occupation unknown, then by his widow, and later by his son, also John Starkey.

By the time the Starkeys left it the house was in need of repair. When Thomas Willington bought it in 1780 he pulled it down and rebuilt in brick. The new house was larger than the old and included a shop. It was double fronted and three storeyed. On the ground floor, the parlour and the shop faced the street with the sitting room and 'tea room' behind them. On the upper floors were seven bedrooms and at the rear a yard with a kitchen, a large bakehouse with an oven, a small barn where wood and kindling for the oven was stored, stables and a pig sty. The first tenant of the new property was Thomas Brookes, a baker, who seems to have also bought the freehold before he retired in 1802.

He sold the property to Humphrey Perry, another baker, who carried on business there until his death in 1824. His widow Elizabeth continued the business until January 1826, when she put the property and business up for sale by auction. In the auctioneer's words, it was 'a modern house near the centre of town, where a bakery business has been carried on for 50 years'. When the property was not sold, Elizabeth carried on for another three years. She then let the house and bakery to Edward Moreton, a baker and dealer in flour. He employed two men to assist him in the bakery and a young girl to help his wife in the shop. All three employees lived-in. In May 1856 Moreton went bankrupt and his stock of flour, together with his household furniture were sold to pay his creditors. A week later the freehold of the property was also advertised for sale, with a note that it was capable of improvement at small cost.

The new owner made extensive alterations, enlarging the shop and putting in a new doorway and a large shop window that projected a little into the street. The premises ceased to be a bakery. The changes can be seen in the earliest photograph on Greengate Street reproduced on page 40.

Late in 1856 Charles Wright opened a drapery and millinery shop there and stayed until 1859. In October 1859 the lease of the premises was taken over by Charles Walker, who had previously had a shop at number 38. He described himself as a mercer, milliner and dealer in straw bonnets, mantles, ladies' dresses, shawls, stays, and baby linen. He was also the local agent for the Alexandra lock-stitch home sewing machine and offered free tuition to anyone who bought one.

In 1867 Walker sold his business to a partnership of Wolley & Cliff. George Wolley, who advertised that he had 22 years experience in the trade, managed the shop and lived on the premises. The shop was large enough to employ five assistants, none of whom lived-in. The business prospered and in February 1872 the partnership 'made extensive alterations to meet the requirements of increasing trade.' Surprisingly, the shop closed in the autumn of the same year and the owner advertised the premises as to let.

The new tenant was R.T.Chandler, linen and woollen draper, who set aside part of the shop as a show room for 'millinery, mantles and the latest fashion novelties'. The business did not attract sufficient custom and went bankrupt at the beginning of 1874. The trustee for the creditors advertised a sale of goods with an invoice value of £1,600.

The shop remained vacant for several months until John Genders opened 'The Exchange Drapery Establishment' there on 1 August 1874. Like R.T.Chandler, he failed to make the business pay and closed his shop after little more than a year.

E.Ward & Sons opened a shop there in October 1875 with a new stock of drapery. But in the following July announced a closing down sale because they were leaving Stafford. However, Thomas Ward, the partner who had been the manager of the shop, decided to take over the business and carried on until the autumn of 1878.

Henry and Joseph Deakin were brothers with a well established tailoring business. They had been forced to move into temporary accomodation in Gaolgate Street in 1875, when their shop was demolished as part of the scheme to improve access to St Chad's church. In November 1878 they moved into number 44. Henry, the elder brother, brought his family to live there and his unmarried younger brother, Joseph, lodged with them. Henry was an acknowledged expert on old books and an accomplished musician. For many years he was the organist at St Chad's church. The brothers' tailoring business was prosperous and employed some twenty out-workers making up and altering garments. They stayed until 1888, when they moved to number 42 Greengate Street.

The next tenant of the shop was Joseph Halden & Son, who were both printers and dealers in china and fancy goods. Joseph Halden had died some years earlier but his son William continued to use the old title for the business. The printing works was in Eastgate Street, where William lived. The business also had show rooms for china and fancy goods in the Borough Hall building.

The new shop brought together and expanded the two sides of the business. There was a glass, china and earthenware department where you could buy Royal Worcester, Coalport, and Minton china as well as everyday ware. In the stationery department you could order printed bill-heads, notices, etc, or buy hymn books, prayer books, writing cases, albums of various kinds and a variety of leather goods, such as purses and gloves. Printing and bookbinding were still carried out at the Eastgate Street works and the business continued to publish its annual directory of Stafford and the neighbouring villages. In 1903 Halden & Son gave up dealing in china and glassware and closed their Greengate Street shop.

After Halden & Son moved out, Arthur

Crinean moved his bakers and confectioners shop from number 37 to number 46. He stayed there for the next ten years. From 1913 to 1933 the premises were occupied by Frederick Kirkham's drapery shop.

For the next 30 years number 46 was Allen's music shop. Edmund Allen had made and sold pianos since 1840. In the late nineteenth century, as pianos became fashionable and every family aspired to have one in their parlour, the business had expanded and branches were opened in Stafford and elsewhere. By 1933 E.F.Allen & Sons sold music and all kinds of musical instruments, as well as having the largest stock of pianos in the town. They claimed to be able to supply 'any make of piano, any style, and at almost any price'. In the early 1960s the shop was taken over by Broadmead Ltd, who carried on their piano and music business there until the late 1960s. The shop was then let to Civic Radio, T.V. and Electrical Ltd. When they moved out in 1974, the premises were left vacant. The upper floor, no longer occupied by the shopkeeper and his family, had been converted into offices. In post-war years, F.Downes' taxi hire business was based there.

In the 1970s the property was bought by the Halifax Building Society, whose architect redesigned the whole building, while retaining much of the frontage above the ground floor. Today the premises are occupied by Halifax plc Bank, the successor of the Halifax Building Society. If you look carefully at the building, you can still see some of the features seen in the earliest photograph of the building on page 40.

Since January 2009 Halifax plc has been part of Lloyds Bank Group.

NUMBER FORTY FIVE - THE SWAN

The traditional story of the beginnings of The Swan as an inn is set out in Roxburgh; Know Your Town - Stafford. He tells how, in 1711, Peter Walley owned two adjacent houses in Greengate Street, one of which was known by the sign of The Swan. By 1752 the two houses had been made into an inn, probably by arching over the gap between them. Further research has now revealed an earlier chapter in its history.

The earliest known reference to The Swan is in 1606, when Thomas Allen senior paid the town chamberlains a rent of three shillings 'for the house he dwelleth in called The Swan, being the land of Mr Barber.' Mr Barber was probably William Barber, gentleman, who owned other property in the town. Chamberlains' rents were annual payments levied on anyone whose property encroached on town land, including the streets. It is not clear what Thomas Allen was paying for, but the amount suggests it was more than a minor encroachment on the street. In the early eighteeth century Peter Walley was paying an identical rent, evidence of continuity from the days of Thomas Allen.

William Barber sold the property to William Ironmonger, who continued to rent it out. Thomas Allen died in February 1610 and was followed by Humphrey Bourne. Bourne's name is variously spelled Bourne, Burne and even Browne, but the spelling Bourne, used in his will, has been adopted here. Bourne described himself as a baker and in 1614, and again in 1615, was fined for selling underweight loaves. However, he had a second occupation. In 1614 he was described as an innholder and baker and a year later he was said to 'keep a common inn and bake horsebread within the same.' Horsebread was poor quality bread, often fed to animals. This is the earliest evidence that ale was being sold at The Swan. In 1614 Bourne failed to give sureties that he would not allow drunkards, the playing of illegal games, or disorderly behaviour on his premises and, as a result, was fined in May 1615 for having an unlicensed alehouse or tippling house.

Bourne was a much married man. His first wife, Margery Baylie, whom he married in 1587, bore him his only son, Humphrey junior. Humphrey junior grew up to be the town's first known fishmonger. He died unexpectedly in 1630 at the age of 41. On his deathbed he made a nuncupative will leaving all his goods and estate to his wife, with the words, 'If it were more it were too little'. Margery Bourne died in May 1597 and in August 1598 Bourne remarried. His second wife was Anne, widow of Jervis Walton and mother of Isaak Walton, whose fifth birthday was the day after the wedding. Humphrey Bourne may not have been at The Swan until 1610, by which time Isaak was an apprentice in London. His mother died in May 1622 but Humphrey Bourne maintained a good relationship with his stepson and in his will left 'Isaak Walton, citizen of London' twenty shillings to buy a memorial ring. After the death of Anne, Bourne remarried. His third wife, Isobel, died in August 1634. Soon afterwards he married for a fourth time. His bride was Susan Bradshaw, who was considerably younger than her new husband. When Humphrey died in 1639, she took over his business as a baker and alehouse keeper.

From the inventory attached to Humphrey

Bourne's will we can learn something about The Swan in the first half of the seventeenth century. The house was timber-framed, with two storeys and a straggle of outbuildings at the rear. The plan was oldfashioned, suggesting that this was an old building. It was of medium size and the furnishings show that Bourne was well-to-do but not rich.

The outer door led into a large hall furnished with two long tables, benches and stools. A pair of playing tables were marked out for games like backgammon and draughts. The room was panelled with oak wainscot and heated by a large open fire in a brick hearth. This was probably the room where ale was served. Next to the hall was the great parlour, the main family room, with a four-poster bed at one end. A long table had a bench along one side. Scattered round the room were a side table, stools and rush-seated chairs, chests, boxes and presses, which held valuables, linen and clothes. Four satin and two dozen other cushions were scattered about and there was a small looking glass on the wall. Other ground floor rooms included a little parlour; a plainly furnished maids' parlour; a kitchen with brass kettles and pots and a large fireplace where spits could stand on cob-irons in front of the fire; and new and old butteries for storing food. Upstairs were six bedchambers, one called The Swan chamber and another used to store malt and oats. At the rear, was a two-storeyed bakehouse with a large oven; a covered store for wood and gorse (used to light the oven); a yelding house where ale was brewed; and a stable.

After carrying on the business for a year, Susan Bourne married John Felton, who came to live at The Swan. Both he and his wife were ardent Royalists. When Parliamentary forces occupied Stafford in 1643, during the Civil War, both Felton and his wife were declared undesirables, who were only to be allowed into the town with a licence. This must have been given, since in February 1644 Felton was ordered to leave the town because he was suspected of passing information about troop movements there to the enemy. He returned later in the year but in October his wife Susan was declared a "malignant" and the couple were told to dispose of their household goods and make the best arrangements they could for their property before leaving the town.

John Felton and his wife returned to Stafford at the end of the Civil War and in 1651 were again recorded as paying three shillings to the town chamberlains 'for the lower part of The Swan'. At some time before his death in the late 1650s John Felton also seems to have bought the freehold of the property. The Swan was inherited by John Felton's son, John Felton junior, who had set up in business as a bookseller and stationer in the market place. He was more prosperous than his father, became a town councillor in 1653 and was chosen as mayor in 1670. After his father's death, he continued to live above his shop and seems to have let The Swan.

There is much uncertainty about the history of the property for the next 50 years. F. W.B.Charles, an expert on seventeenth century buildings, dated the core of the present Swan building to the middle years of the seventeenth century, adding that it would have been one of the first brick buildings in the town. The Swan was therefore rebuilt by one of the Feltons. John Felton junior was more wealthy than his father and is more likely to have carried out the work. The building would thus date from the 1660s. In 1662 John Felton junior paid the usual three shillings to the town chamberlains but was also due to pay 'for late outbuilding the house and shop and for his sign post there'. The extra amount due had not been fixed and was never added onto the three shillings. Is this evidence of rebuilding The Swan or is it a charge for work done on John Felton's shop in the market place? The form of the chamberlains' accounts and the loss of all late seventeenth century assessments makes it impossible to be sure. Neither can we be certain whether The Swan continued to be both bakery and alehouse until it was rebuilt.

The Swan was rebuilt as two houses, both of which were let to tenants. When John Felton junior died in 1685 he left The Swan to his son Thomas and the 'other messuage adjoining The Swan Inn and now in the occupation of William Bradshaw' to his daughter Anne. The Swan had been let to John Harrison and Thomas Felton continued to let it. He was noted as the owner of the property in 1704 and probably continued to own The Swan until 1711. During those years there is no evidence as to the use to which the premises were put, although it is a reasonable assumption that they continued to be an inn.

In 1711 Peter Walley, an apothecary in the town, bought both The Swan and the adjacent house, which are described as in the occupation of Joseph Parsons and Elizabeth Dodd, widow. Walley mortgaged the properties to Humphrey Hodgetts for £200. In 1723 a second mortgage for £80 was taken out and in 1725 a third mortgage for £60. By 1752 Walley's daughter Anne had inherited the properties and moved to Lichfield. She was unable to redeem the mortgages and sold the properties to John Hodgetts, who held all three mortgages. By the time of the sale 'the two messuages were lain into one, commonly called The Swan Inn'.

The change can be dated fairly precisely. When Peter Walley bought the two properties in 1711, he lived in the house and rented The Swan to a tenant. A Land Tax assessment in 1732 and a rate levied to raise money to build a workhouse for the poor in Stafford in 1735 both show that there were still two properties. However, a Land Tax assessment in 1742 shows a single property. The change can therefore be dated as between 1735 and 1742 with 1737, when the chamberlains rent payable on The Swan was changed, as a probable date. By that time Peter Walley had died and his widow had moved out of the house adjacent to the inn.

The tenant of the inn was William Butt from some time before 1729. In 1741 he retired and made an agreement with his eldest son, also William Butt, who had just married Alice Hayes the daughter of a Lichfield apothecary, that William junior would take over the inn and pay his father a small annuity. The new tenant did not stay long. In 1746 he was replaced by William Godwin, who remained until 1757.

In 1757 John Hodgetts leased the inn to Robert Sylvester. Sylvester was young and ambitious. He was the son of Robert Sylvester senior, one of the town's capital burgesses, who had been mayor in 1755. In 1779 Sylvester bought the freehold of The Swan from John Hodgetts with the intention of making it one of the leading inns in the town.

He leased, and later bought, land behind the inn from Lord Stafford in order to extend the inn yard and build additional stables and outbuildings to house chaises. Travellers could hire a chaise with horses and a driver. Sylvester rented a riverside meadow (now part of Victoria Park) to provide hay for the horses in his stables. When a public coach providing a four-times-a-day service between Manchester and Birmingham was started in the 1780s the coaches stopped at The Swan to change horses.

The inn itself was also modernised. In 1786 the first bow window facing Greengate Street was added to the inn. As modernisation continued, a second bow window was added in 1788 and a third in 1793. Sylvester was careful to appoint good staff. An advertisement for a woman cook insisted on a recommendation 'for honesty, sobriety, attention and cleanliness'. It added that 'one upwards of thirty, who has lived in at a reputable inn, will be more approved'. The Hon John Byng, who visited the town in 1792, found all the inns rather like alehouses, full of market people, but conceded that The Swan was the best of them. The inn was bustling with farmers on market days, with attorneys and gentlemen on county and court business when the county magistrates were sitting, and with visitors from as far afield as London during Race Week.

After Robert Sylvester died in 1799, The Swan, described as 'an inn of the first consequence', was sold by auction. The new owner was Thomas Webster, who paid £1580, as well as taking all the furniture, wine, liquor, chaises and horses at valuation. Webster took out a large mortgage for £1000 and with the interest to be paid, found his profits less than expected. In March 1803 he accepted an offer from Lord Stafford to buy the inn for £700 plus taking over the mortgage. In return Webster agreed to stay on as licensee for the time being.

When Webster left in 1805, the Stafford estate advertised for a new tenant for the inn and 70 acres of rich meadow. In the words of the advertisement, 'The inn has lately undergone a thorough repair and improvement both internally and externally and is superior to any other inn in the town.' The new tenant was John Hughes, who was already the licensee of The Star Inn in the market place. He managed both inns for the next 20 years. He seems to have concentrated provision for public coaches at The Star. By 1818 only the twice daily post-coach between Manchester and Birmingham changed horses at The Swan and by 1820 this had also been transferred to The Star. However, The Swan expanded its hire of private chaises and other vehicles. Hughes retired in 1826.

The next tenant was William Sirdefield, who left in 1833, after Lord Stafford had refused to agree to improvements that he wanted to make at the inn. The inn was then let to John Meeson, a local man and the younger brother of William Meeson, a considerable boot and shoe manufacturer. John Meeson made a determined effort to attract coaches to The Swan.

Coach proprietors made contracts with innkeepers along their routes to provide fresh horses and care for those taken out of the coach. On its return journey the coach horses were changed back to those used on the outward journey. The innkeeper was paid an agreed sum for each double mile his horses had pulled the coach. Coaches stopped only long enough to change horses, so those who travelled on them added little to an innkeeper's trade, but those waiting for a coach or alighting from one would often dine at the inn, or hire a chaise for an onward journey, or stay the night if they had business in the town.

By 1834 John Meeson had negotiated contracts to supply horses to all the mail-coaches travelling between Birmingham and either Manchester or Liverpool. Every day 12 coaches stopped to change horses and pick up passengers. With four horses required for each coach, the inn stables were full. These were the busiest years for The Swan as a coaching inn.

During this time George Borrow, the author of Romany Rye, worked as an ostler at The Swan for a few weeks. His account conveys a picture of the busy inn, although at times autobiography is blended with fiction. 'The inn,' he wrote, 'was a place of infinite life and bustle. Travellers of all descriptions were continually stopping at it, and to attend to their wants and minister to their convenience, an army of servants was kept; waiters, chambermaids, grooms, postillions, shoe-blacks, cooks, scullions, and what not, for there was a barber and hairdresser who had been at Paris and talked French with a Cockney accent. Jacks creaked in the kitchens, turning spits on which large joints of meat smoked and piped. There was running up and down stairs, slamming of doors, cries of 'Coming, Sir', and 'Please to step this way, ma'am,' during eighteen hours of the four and twenty. Truly a very great place for life and bustle was this inn.'

The opening of the railway through Stafford in 1837 led to all long distance coaches through the town being taken off the road. They were unable to compete either on speed or price. Only coaches running cross-country to towns not yet served by the railway survived. The Swan still provided a daily mail-coach to Lichfield and coaches to Newcastle and Newport. John Meeson also provided an omnibus to meet every train at the station and convey passengers to the inn. The end of the coaching era brought a rapid decline in the fortunes of The Swan.

When Charles Dickens visited Stafford in 1852 he stayed one night at The Swan. 'The extinct Town-inn, the Dodo', he called it. 'The Dodo's habits are all wrong. It provides me with a trackless desert of sitting room, with a chair for every day of the year, a table for every month, and a waste of sideboard, where a lonely china vase pines for its mate, long departed. The Dodo has nothing in the larder. Even now I perceive the boots returning with the sole for my supper in a piece of paper. Seeing me at the blank bow window, he slaps his legs as he comes across the road, pretending it is something else. The waiter cleans the table and draws the dingy curtains of the great bow window, which so unwillingly meet that they must be pinned together. When I mount up to my bedroom, a smell of closeness and flue gets lazily up my nose like sleepy snuff. The loose bits of carpet writhe under my tread, and take wormy shapes. The Dodo is narrow minded as to towels; it expects me to wash on a freemason's apron without the trimmings; when I ask for soap, gives me a stony hearted something white with no more lather in it than the Elgin marbles. The Dodo has seen better days and possesses interminable stables at the back - silent, grass-grown, broken-windowed and horseless.'

Changes in the needs of travellers after the coming of railways led to the decline of the large town inn. Of three great inns in the centre of Stafford at the beginning of the nineteenth century, only The Swan survived by 1854, when John Meeson retired after more than 20 years at the inn.

The new licensee was Frederick Wood, the licensee of The Eagle on Newport Road. He attempted to revive the inn by increasing its use for balls and town functions. In December 1855 he opened a new assembly room at The Swan with a magnificent ball, attended by 150 guests described by The Staffordshire Advertiser as 'beauty and fashion'. The room was decorated with flags and evergreens and, suspended at one end, a large Stafford knot outlined by gas jets. A buffet supper had been laid on in the old assembly room and Tilley's quadrille band played until 5 o'clock the next morning.

In 1866 Wood built The North Western Railway Hotel opposite the station to cater for travellers by rail. He managed both hotels until 1871, when he gave up the tenancy of The Swan. The omnibus from the hotel continued to meet every train, chaises and other equipages were still available on hire, and, in addition, hearses and funeral carriages with black horses could be hired there.

After Wood left, James Senior, licensee of the Vine in Salter Street, became the tenant. He managed both premises until 1885, when he retired, having done nothing to halt the slow decline of The Swan. The next tenant was H.J.Mundy who set about making the hotel more attractive with new commercial and billiard rooms and a clear out of old and surplus coaches. Among the coaches disposed of were a four-horse stage coach, 3 omnibuses, 3 broughams, 2 landaus, 1 hansom cab, 1 barouche, 6 dog carts and a four wheeled phaeton. Only the most modern coaches were retained. He also sold off eight 'seasoned horses'. Munday stayed only a short time and was followed by a succession of equally shortlived licensees.

In the twentieth century the hotel gained new custom from motorists and cyclists. As early as 1903 part of the stabling was converted into garages, although broughams, phaetons, wagonettes, dog carts, funeral and weddding equipages were still available for hire.

THE "SWAN" HOTEL, STAFFORD.

This well-known County Hotel, situated in the main street, and within three minutes' walk of the Railway Station, has recently passed under new management, and been thoroughly renovated.

PRIVATE SITTING ROOMS, a very large ASSEMBLY ROOM (suitable for Balls, Public Dinners, &c), COFFEE, READING, COMMERCIAL, and BILLIARD ROOMS.

EXCELLENT STABLING AND COACH-HOUSES.

POSTING IN ALL ITS BRANCHES.

GOOD CUISINE, WINE, AND ATTENDANCE.

TERMS MODERATE.

1886. H. J. MUNDY, Manager.

Advertisement for The Swan in 1886

The Swan in the early twentieth century.

Loose boxes for horses continued to be provided until the 1920s.

In 1928/9 a major renovation of the hotel took place. The archway that had provided access to the stables and garages at the rear was closed in and became an entrance hall with steps to Greengate Street. Inside the hotel, the old lounge and a private room to the left of the entrance hall became the new dining room. The grille room on the other side of the hall was converted into a lounge. New toilets were built and a modern central heating system installed. At the rear, part of the old stable block was demolished to provide a better access to the garages from Mill Street. Other changes were made in the 1930s and 1940s to meet the changing demands of those using the hotel.

In 1954 there was a major threat to The Swan. Sidney Hall, the licensee, had bought the hotel from the Stafford estate in 1950. Four years later he sold it to Ind, Coope & Allsopp, and bought Tillington Hall to convert into an hotel. The new owners of The Swan proposed to take away the licence and convert the building into shops and offices. Their proposals aroused considerable opposition in the town. The Borough Council placed a preservation order on the building and refused to sanction a change of use.

The hotel remained open and a popular manager built up its reputation as a bar and meeting place. An employee of the time recalled, 'The hotel offered three bars. The George Borrow Bar was stark, white-washed and had a minstrels' gallery. It was used by young people and students and got very raucous on Saturday night. The Oak Room, on the left of the entrance, featured the dark heavy panelling removed from Stafford Castle. It was used largely by local businessmen. The American Bar, on the right of the entrance, was 'up market' and furnished with easy chairs and sofas. It served cocktails and various bourbons but sold no draught beer, only bottled - regarded at the time as very posh.'

Musical entertainment was provided by local performers such as Reg Shakespeare, who played the banjo and always had his dog called The Vicar with him. Other musicians included The Winnie Grundy Band and the blind pianist Norman Green and his trio. The Swan was also the home of the Stafford Modern Jazz Club, which met in the Borrow Bar. As the popularity of folk music grew in the 1960s, The Swan nurtured the formation of The Cygnet Folk Club. This was run by Ron Winkle, who did so in exchange for the use of vacant stables at the rear of the hotel as a place where he could work on vintage motor cars. Friday night was Folk Night. The club, which at one time had over 200 members, met in the first floor Green Room.

By the 1990s The Swan was in need of refurbishment and the expectations of potential customers had changed. In November 2001 the then owners, The Scottish and Newcastle Brewery, sold it to the Lewis family, who already owned the Moat House Hotel at Acton Trussell. They closed the hotel to allow a complete face-lift to be carried out. When the hotel reopened in 2002, the ground floor was divided into a number of distinct areas - coffee bar, cocktail bar, sun terrace, bar and brasserie. The brasserie would seat over a hundred people and was open for meals until 10 pm. New conference rooms were also created and a walled garden where live gigs could be staged in the summer months. Further improvements followed. At the end of 2008 the 31 bedrooms were given new luxury bathrooms, flat-screen television and wi-fi internet access.

During the alterations a number of original features were discovered hidden behind plaster. These have been carefully preserved.

NUMBER FORTY SIX - SHAW'S HOUSE

This large timber-framed house stands between The Swan and The High House. It was built by an unknown, but wealthy, Stafford family in the first half of the sixteenth century and is at least 50 years older than The High House. When it was built, it had three storeys, with the topmost open to the roof, but during the seventeenth century the rooms on the top floor were given ceilings, and garrets formed above them. These were lit by inserting windows in each of the two gable ends. Beneath the house was a large stone basement or cellar which raised the ground floor some feet above street level, so that it had to be reached by steps that encroached on Greengate Street. On the south side of the house, a passage provided access from the street to the garden and outbuildings at the rear.

For the first 200 years of the house's history nothing is known about those who owned or inhabited it. The first person known to have lived there was Charles Wedgwood in the 1720s. Wedgwood described himself as a gentleman and this was a gentleman's residence. Wedgwood, and later his widow, lived in the house until 1735. It was then bought by William Foden, a member of a well-to-do legal family. He died in 1741, but his widow survived him and lived in the house for another 16 years.

In 1757 Widow Foden's executors sold the house to William Bickley. He was a cabinet maker and the son of John Bickley of Rugeley, who was also a cabinet maker. William was in his early thirties when he came to Stafford. In the mid-eighteenth century mahogany furniture in new, elegant styles was replacing older and more solid pieces. Cabinet makers and their well-to-do customers were influenced by pattern books showing the latest styles. Thomas Chippendale's 'The Gentleman and Cabinet Maker's Directory' had been published only three years before Bickley bought the house in Greengate Street. He set out to meet the demands of prosperous tradesmen in the town, and to encourage them to commission from him furniture in the latest fashion.

During his ownership, the house was improved by fitting a new staircase. Careful examination of it at a later date showed that Bickley had used a staircase removed from another building and skilfully adapted it to fit his house. About the same time, a new portico with stone pillars was built over the steps up to the front door. The outside of the house was plastered at this time to make it more waterproof and the plaster painted with a design in black and white, that imitated the pattern of timber framing on the High House.

William Bickley died in 1787 but his widow continued to live in the house until her death in March 1796 and his unmarried daughter was there until 1799. In those days the Corporation had to provide accomodation for the judges who came to the town each year to hold the assizes. The rooms had to be quiet, private and of a standard acceptable to professional men. An inn was not suitable. In the late eighteenth century the Bickley's house was used, although it had some drawbacks. One magistrate wrote that the 'rooms were ill adapted to dine 30 or 40 and were always very crowded on account of their small size, though perhaps the best that the town could offer'.

Number 46 based on a drawing by
John Ferneyhough, 1823.

After Miss Bickley left in 1799, 'the judges were turned out of their old, petty lodging box'. The house seems to have been vacant for about a year, with taxes paid by agents. In 1801 it was sold to Henry Webb, the senior partner in Stevenson, Webb and Stevenson Bank in Market Square. He let it to Mrs Hand, a widow, until 1805. By that time the bank building, where he was living, was about to be demolished and rebuilt. Webb moved into the Greengate Street house although his mistress, with whom he had been living for more than ten years, continued to occupy a house on The Green with her eight children. He moved easily among county society and was appointed High Sheriff in 1810.

A plan of the house during Webb's ownership, now in The William Salt Library, shows that the main door led into a square hall, with Webb's office behind it, having a view over the garden. On the right of the hall was the parlour, with a view of Greengate Street, and, behind the parlour, the kitchen and other domestic rooms. The sitting room was on the first floor over the parlour. The bedrooms and rooms for servants occupied the rest of the upper floors.

Henry Webb lived in the house until about 1816, when he bought Forebridge Hall (now Green Hall) on Lichfield Road.The Greengate Street house was let to Sarah Princep briefly and then occupied by his eldest daughter. She died in 1823. Henry's mistress died in the same year. He then married Rachel Garrett, a widow who had been the matron at Coton Hill Asylum. They lived at the hall. Webb's elder son, Charles Henry Webb, training to be an attorney, moved into Greengate Street and lived there until his father died in 1831. He then moved into Forebridge Hall, which he had inherited, and his step-mother moved into the Greengate Street house, where she died in April 1833.

After Rachel Webb's death, the house was sold to Robert Hughes, the second son of Dr Francis Hughes, surgeon at The Staffordshire General Infirmary. He had been named after his grandfather, Robert Hughes, an apothecary who had been the first Secretary to the Board at the infirmary. The younger Robert, born in 1803, had acted as his father's assistant before completing his medical training in London. In 1830 he had been appointed surgeon at Wolverhampton Dispensary. At the beginning of 1833 his father had announced his retirement from his post at The Staffordshire General Infirmary and Robert had successfully applied to succeed him. He moved back to Stafford, bought the house in Greengate Street and lived there until 1842.

When he moved out, the house was extensively altered and made into a shop with living accomodation at the rear and on the upper floors. The plastered frontage was painted white and left plain; the pillared portico was taken down; the parlour was converted into a shop with a new display window built out under the first floor overhang. Upstairs, the sitting room was given a new bay window overlooking Greengate Street. The new shop would be let.

William Shaw was a saddler. In 1831 he had taken over a saddler's shop at 54 Greengate Street and added a china and glassware department managed by his wife. In April 1841

Number 46 from a print 'Old Houses, Greengate Street' published by R. & W. Wright in 1859. The picture grossly exaggerates the height of the building in comparison with its width.

his wife, who was only 29 years old, died suddenly, leaving a young family. Shaw was deeply distressed. He sold off all the china and glassware and moved to a smaller shop in Market Square. By 1843 he had recovered and rented the new shop at number 46. In his first advertisement for his saddlery and leather goods shop he announced that, now he had more commodious premises, part of them would be 'fitted up with a stock of china, glass and earthenware at prices that cannot fail to give satisfaction'. At first his business struggled to survive. In January 1844 he was forced into a sale of stock to raise money to pay his creditors, but, by the following May he was again solvent and thanking his customers for their support. By the end of the 1840s he had ceased to deal in china and about 1850 opened a general groceries counter in his saddler's shop. He retired in 1872 and his son William Daniel Shaw carried on the business. In June 1877, when the property was put up for sale, William Shaw bought it. The building was occupied by the family for so many years that it has become known as Shaw's House.

Major alterations to the building were carried out in 1891, after William Daniel Shaw had bought a house on the outskirts of the town and moved his family out of number 46. The old entrance and steps up to the house were removed and the ground floor lowered to near street level. The existing shop was refurbished and a second shop created at the southern end of the building. The second shop was given the address 45A and its history is related on page 74. Not long afterwards, the vacant upstairs rooms were taken over by The Swan as additional bedrooms and access from the hotel made on the first floor. William Daniel Shaw continued to occupy his shop at number 46 until he retired in 1898.

After he retired, a new type of tea and grocery shop opened at number 46. Previously, grocers had selected what they sold, relying on their experience to judge quality and fix prices. In the late nineteenth century companies began to open numerous branch shops, each selling the same goods, in the same packaging, at the same price. Shops were put in charge of managers whose job was simply selling. In 1898 number 46 became one of Thomas Lipton & Co's 245 branch shops selling grocery and especially tea. The company remained there until they moved to Gaolgate Street Street in 1921.

Since 1921 the shop has housed a variety of retailers. From 1921 to 1926 it was T.E. Baker & Co, clothiers and tailors. In 1926 the premises were refitted as a temporary branch of The National and Provincial Bank, while their Market Square premises were being rebuilt. In 1928 it became a chemist's shop run by B.E.Jones, who had bought the goodwill of Fowke & Son's business in Market Square when Woolworth's took over Fowke's premises. By 1930 this was Taylor's Cash Chemists and in the 1940s Timothy White & Taylor, chemists.

In 1947 the plaster on the front of the building was removed to reveal fairly plain timber framing. After the plaster had been renewed, it was painted with a black and white pattern in imitation of timber framing. But, instead of copying the genuine framing, a more elaborate pattern was adopted. In the 1960s the design was blocked out when the front was repainted.

In 1961 Timothy White & Taylor , who had another shop in Market Square, closed their Greengate Street branch. It was still vacant in 1962, when W.H.Smith & Son's premises on the other side of the street were badly damaged by fire. Smith's took over the building and moved some of their departments into it while the fire damage was repaired.

Since W.H.Smith & Son moved out, the premises have been occupied by a succession of businesses. In 1970 it was Bellman's knitting wool shop. Five years later it was

Tiko's cafe and then, in the 1980s, Wimbush's British Bakery and self-service cafe. About 1990 it was opened by the Three Cooks chain as a confectionery shop and restaurant. The shop closed in September 2007 when the chain went into administration. In January 2008 the premises were taken over by the Lewis Partnership, which owned The Swan, and opened as a delicatessen with a policy of championing fine food from local sources. Number 46 is now The Greengate Deli.

Numbers 46 and 45A about 1950

NUMBER FORTY FIVE A

In 1891 the first tenant of this new shop was Emily Dobson, who opened a tobacconist's shop there and stayed until about 1898. Sidney Taylor then bought the lease and converted the premises into a music shop. He sold pianos, organs and gramophones, as well as tuning and repairing instruments. He also stocked sheet music and established a music library from which anyone who paid half a guinea to join could borrow sheet music for a small fee. He was also a concert agent, who supplied artistes and bands for dances,garden parties and other entertainments. He sold the business to W.H.Priestley & Sons in 1909 and they carried on their music shop there until the lease expired in March 1921.

After the music shop closed, The Lancashire and Cheshire Rubber Company sold mackintoshes and oilskins there for a short time.

In 1924 the premises were taken by Fleming, Reid & Co, a group of worsted spinners and hosiers, selling all sorts of knitted garments direct to the public at factory prices. The shop was later renamed The Scotch Wool and Hosiery Stores. The company remained there for over 40 years.

In the late 1960s, when the Scotch Wool shop closed, the shop became James Baker's shoe shop. In 1985 this was taken over and became Clarke's Shoes. After the shoe shop closed, the premises remained vacant for a time until The Capital Appliance Centre moved in, selling cut-price electrical appliances such as washing machines and cookers. After they left in 1998, the shop was vacant until The Peoples Dispensary for Sick Animals opened a charity shop there in 1999.

PRINCIPAL GENERAL SOURCES

Local and County Directories 1783-1970
Kemp: Freemen of Stafford Borough 1100-1997
Staffordshire Newsletter
Staffordshire Advertiser
Stafford chamberlains' rents 1699-1704 and
1729-1835 (SRO D(W) 0/8/2-3, D1033/1,
D1323/E/2)
Land Tax Assessments 1732-1832 with many gaps.
(WSL 7/00/87-9; SRO D1798/618/142 & 231,
GRP/1)
Stafford Poor Rate, 1768 (WSL 7/00/86)
Census enumerators books 1841-1901
Ordance Survey 1/500 map of Stafford, 1879
Goad Maps from 1969

ADDITIONAL SOURCES FOR SOME PROPERTIES

Number 36
Chetwynd-Stapleton: The Chetwynds of
Ingestre (1892)
Lewis: Stafford Shoes (1984)
Amphlett: The Newspaper Press (1860)
SRO D1798/618/163 (Riots of 1747)
WSL 788/36, 843/36, 888/36 (leases) and
7/100/166 (sale catalogue)

Numbers 37 - 40
Victor: Widow of the Wood (1755)
Byrne: The Widow of the Wood (1964)
Roxburgh: Know Your Town - Stafford (1948)
The chapter on the District Bank confuses
deeds relating to numbers 40 and 41
SRO D1798 HM26/1 & 2 (Perry notebooks),
D1798 HM32, D1798/664/24-33 (leases),
D1798/666/193 (Robins inventory, 1754),
D1798/666/16 (Robins settlement 1760)

Number 42
The sources for Omar Hall and a more detailed
account of his early career are in number

1 of this series 'From High House to Bakers Oven' (57 Greengate Street)

Number 43
SRO D1798 HM 26/1 & 2, D1798/666/90 (Perry)

Number 44
SRO D1798/666/90 (lease in 1731)
The Humphrey Perry of this chapter is not related to the Humphrey Perry on pages 13 and 41.

Number 45
Roxburgh: Know Your Town - Stafford (1948)
Pennington and Rootes: The Committee at Stafford 1643-5 (SHC 4th series vol 1)
Kettle: Matthew Craddock's Book of Remembrance (SHC 4th series vol 16)
Borrow : Romany Rye (1857)
Dickens: A Plated Article
Its Swanderful (Staffs Newsletter 24.6.04)
WSL 854/36 (sale and mortgage), OS 402 (copies of seventeenth century town rents, etc)
SRO D641/3/A/5/1/1-6 (Sale and lease). There are other leases in D641/3
SRO D1798/685/352 (Butt family agreement)
LRO Will of Humphrey Bourne senior 22.3.1638/) and John Felton 22.9. 1685

Number 46
Wrottesley: Narrative of the fact ....Judges lodgings (1811)
Charles: Survey Report on the High House (1975)
WSL M516 (Plan of house)

ABBREVIATIONS
LRO Lichfield Record Office
SRO Staffordshire County Record Office
WSL William Salt Library